D1561024

# 170 Questions For A Successful

# First Date

Gunthar Fleck

Everyone has an anecdote about that one first date they went on. Perhaps it was a catastrophe of biblical proportions where the date had horrible breath, talked about their obsession with an ex-partner, told terribly dry stories that made time stand still, insisted that you pay for everything, spoke with their mouth full, did not speak at all, dropped a magnum condom on the table when opening their wallet, did not look like their profile picture, turned out to be a second cousin only realized after the first kiss. They could have stood too tall, too short, too easy, or too pious. Or maybe, the first dates that come to mind are ones of love or chemistry at first sight. And good for those people for getting the best out of the experience. Whatever you think of when you hear the term "first date" you know it is a universal event in which much of the free world can relate to.

We have all witnessed them – either firsthand or in the wild. They are as inevitable as death and taxes. Even eavesdropping on a first date in a bar or restaurant can be such a simple pleasure. We are creatures of curiosity when it comes to romantic interactions. Voyeurs for the delights that we have or hope to experience. These events are vulnerable, yet they largely occur in public. Why do we do this? Why has the concept of dating not changed with the evolution of modern society? Sure, we know about Netflix and Chill. We know about hookups, prostitution, arranged marriages, casual encounters, friends with benefits, and the occasional hermit that sees no value in building a relationship. But for the most part, dates occur when two people meet to get to know each other. They want to see if there is an attraction on a physical, emotional, and sometimes spiritual level. First dates seek to optimize compatibility for longevity with someone.

It sounds excruciatingly painful. And we know sometimes we would rather have teeth pulled or our eyeballs lit ablaze than sit across from someone for the better part of an evening and make conversation. In this handy little guide, I seek to create a helpful assortment of questions intended to get to know someone on a first date. These questions can be tough, or they can be playful. Sometimes they are downright direct. Other times they are indirect to glean more than what was said. Reading between the lines. The art of deduction can be powerful in finding out the nature of a date's tendencies, history, and motives. People are scary, but first dates shouldn't be. That is why the following list of questions should ease the burden of extroversion mandatory for continuing the progress of man in a monogamous society. Without first dates, the world might not continue. The threat of stability within the classic nuclear family formula could upend everyday life as we know it.

The world is already fragile, and you are part of something bigger now. The questions that come will have reasoning below it. This will be helpful for you to get to know the person you are on a date with. Try to chart out goals and envision a future. The resiliency of understanding your date is the key. With that, get out there! Have fun! And, most importantly, don't mess up!

Wikimedia Commons

Gunthar Fleck

# The Classics

What Netflix shows are you watching? What's the difference between Netflix and Hulu? Is there any superiority between the two? Which demographics prefer one over the other do you think?

*The age-old ice breaker. Get to know your date with what shows they are watching. Maybe this will kick up a simple, organic conversation in which mutual interests align.*

Evert F. Baumgardner - National Archives and Records Administration.

Gunthar Fleck

Do you believe in ghosts? If not, how could you be so confident if you have never seen one? If

you have seen one, what happened?

*Regardless of how they answer, proceed to go into detail of your favorite ghost story. True or*

*not.*

Wikimedia Commons

Who is the most famous person you have met? How was the interaction with them? Were they a

- stuck-up celebrity? Or was it someone you got to know personally?

*Don't pry too much as this could lead to an example where sexual history comes up and ruins*

*your date.*

Wikimedia Commons

What is one thing you could never live without? Maybe it's something you can buy anywhere or

maybe it's a personal keepsake? What if I told you, you never need to worry about that necessity

again, because you'll have everything you need with me?


*This comes off as confident, but if you stumble over your words as you say it, you are likely to*

*come across as endearing.*

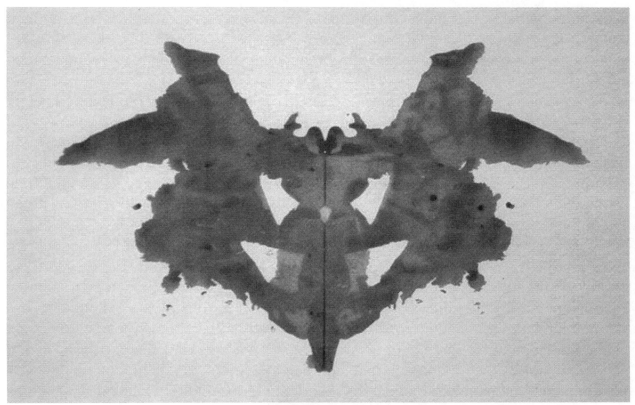

Wikimedia Commons

If you could go back in time, when would you go? Do you think a time machine would work better with uranium power or some energy source we have not harnessed yet? Do you think if you went back to a different time and place, the language barrier would be frustrating?

*Science is a powerful subject to discuss. Not many people are equipped with empirical evidence, however, everyone has opinions which makes for a great flow of conversation on a first date.*

Wikimedia Commons

What did you study in college? Do you use that curriculum in your current work? No, I get you use psychology in everyday life, but do you work in psychology?

*Aspirations are very important. It is worth finding out how often a date's aspirations change. Or at least get a glimpse of the job market for different college majors.*

Wikimedia Commons

Gunthar Fleck

# Passions

Who is your favorite sports team? Are they your favorite because your dad made you watch them growing up? Did your dad get moody if they lost, ultimately leading to you thinking you did something wrong? Which in turn led you to using humor for affirmation that you were still appreciated? Have you ever caught a foul ball/home run at a baseball game?

*This is such an easy, lighthearted topic that will remain in your mind whether the relationship continues or abruptly ends. Each time you see that sports team, you'll be reminded of them in hopefully a sweet way.*

Wikimedia Commons

Have you had a chance to travel much? Where would you recommend going? What would be your dream vacation?

*These are pretty open questions, but WHATEVER you do, do not ask them about their sexual history abroad. Again, past partners being discussed can ruin your night if you have insecurities like most of us do.*

Wikimedia Commons

Have you done any volunteering? Did you find the experience enriching or was it just not something you were passionate about? If you weren't passionate about volunteering, was it for some required community service? Perhaps for a fraternity/sorority? Or some minor infraction like driving while intoxicated, but it was your first time, and your parents had a very good lawyer?

*All these things can give transparency to someone's passions, their upbringing, and true source of value.*

Wikimedia Commons

Have you ever had a collection of something? Where did you get the interest in whatever it was/is you collect? Do you think you started this out of a desire for retention of some tangible value stemming from a deep seeded anxiety that you will never make anything of yourself?

*This conversation is two-fold. First, it shows your date takes up interests beyond social media and sports. Second, if you two collect the same thing, you can merge them down the line.*

Wikimedia Commons

If you could see any concert, past or present, who would you go see? If it's the past, would you

want to see them perform at the age they would be now?

*Obviously, they would choose their prime, but it fills the void of silence because you are running*

*out of things to ask at this point.*

Wikimedia Commons

Gunthar Fleck

Do you enjoy cooking? What's your go-to dish? What inspired you to start cooking? Do you see

yourself cooking with me?


*This is very sensitive information, and it looks bold to ask things like the above. But be bold in*

*the face of social norms.*

Wikimedia Commons

Gunthar Fleck

Have you ever taken an art class? What about art is most inspiring to you? Would you ever go to

an art museum with me?

*Maybe they will discuss their experience being a nude model which equates to promiscuity and*

*the possibility of a kiss after the first date. But be careful, this could lead to you making next date*

*plans to an extremely boring art museum.*

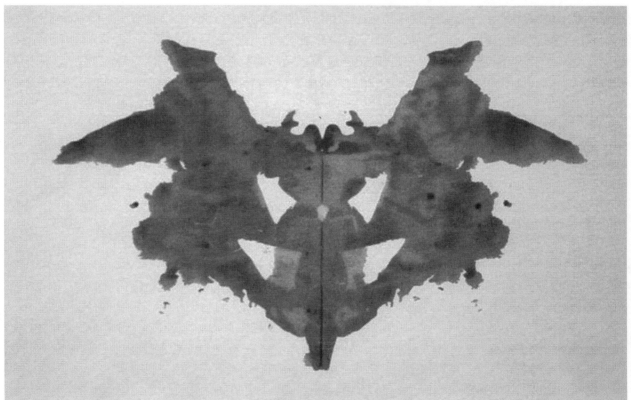

Wikimedia Commons

Gunthar Fleck

# Culture

Gunthar Fleck

Do you think the moon landing was real? Why would the flag be flying in the film despite wind

not existing on the moon? What do you think moon rocks feel like?

*These questions are valid. It shows you do not take anything for face value. It also shows you*

*respect their opinion. Be respectful.*

Wikimedia Commons

Are you on Reddit? If not, why? If so, what are your frequent subreddits? Do you want to give

me your username so I can tag you in funny threads? Coincidentally, do you have an aversion to

NSFW posts?


*Opening a mutual dialogue between interesting subjects on a platform like Reddit could pave the*

*way for efficient communication and resolved understanding at the forefront of a relationship.*

Wikimedia Commons

What was the last good book you read? Have you read anything by Gunthar Fleck? He's a brilliant artist and has round about points that circle the line of funny, but rarely ever cross it. Do you enjoy fiction or non-fiction? If you could loan me any book, what would it be?

*Not necessarily a red flag if they haven't read Fleck but look out for elementary answers from your date.*

Wikimedia Commons

What is it about Banksy that people lose their minds over? What do you think about graffiti artists? Do you think vandalism is cool? What about breaking the law does it for you?

*Picture yourself with someone who likes the idea of a criminal presenting their ludicrous stunts as art. That is not a partner who is equipped to raise a child. It is insane to let these people into your life. I bet they would let a burglar take whatever they wanted. Listen to me, DO NOT TOLERATE THIS LACKADAISICAL PERCEPTION.*

,

Wikimedia Commons

What type of Maduro cigar do you prefer to smoke on Labor Day? Do you think that worker

exhibition should be addressed given inflationary pressures? How high is gasoline going to go?

Do you think you will ever be able to afford a home?

*The idea of home ownership is for those that are out-of-touch lunatics. Search for yourself*

*someone who lives on planet Earth and understands their situation.*

Wikimedia Commons

Do you like podcasts? Would you ever consider starting one? What would you discuss? True crime is commonly saturated, but perhaps you know interesting enough people to have on as guests?

*This is helpful in gauging your date's capacity for pop culture and their eagerness to try new things. If things go well, you may have a new podcast co-host.*

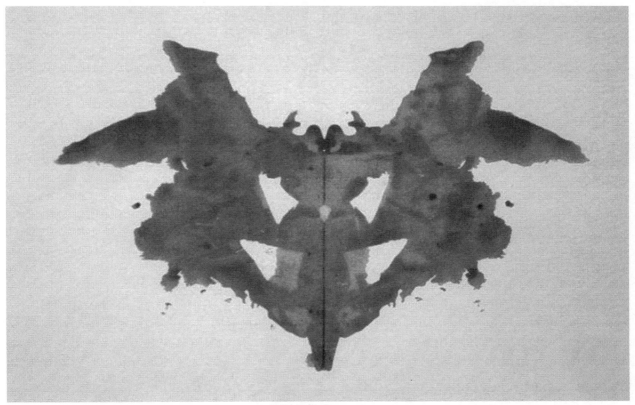

Wikimedia Commons

Do you prefer coffee or tea? What is it about starting the day off with a dose of caffeine that the urgency of bowels being evacuated and hyper-awareness is required?

*If they don't drink either you can be assured they are problematic. If they just drink tea, you can begin to imagine a future where your bedtime becomes 9PM and your Christmases are populated with matching sweaters.*

Wikimedia Commons

Gunthar Fleck

# Health and Wellness

What are your workout habits? Do you focus on agility? Or do you just focus on strength? Have you ever had a personal trainer for fat burning sessions?

*It can be an interesting conversation when someone has an exercise routine, and sometimes it can be unique to learn something new. If they don't have much physical aptitude, it's acceptable to shut down the conversation and change the subject as to not shame the person you are on a date with. If they do work out, this would be a good time to show off your abilities with some push-ups.*

Wikimedia Commons

Gunthar Fleck

Have you ever been in a car accident? Were you at fault? If so, why? Do you have a history of

substance abuse? Do you know anyone who's been in a plane crash? If so, who was at fault?


*Not your usual question asked on a first date, however, it shows that you are not the usual*

*person they date. The robustness of these questions will leave a lasting impact on the person you*

*are sharing the date with.*

Wikimedia Commons

Gunthar Fleck

Do you take naps? Do you take short, power naps? Or do you take long, day ruining, bitchiness

inducing slumbers?

*How a person treats their sleep balance is important. It provides an inside look toward their self-*

*respect.*

Wikimedia Commons

If you were to order ice cream at your favorite shop, what would you get? Why has sorbet not

caught on like we expected it to in the 2000's? Since when did people start including savory

flavors into ice cream? Do you have a favorite memory around eating ice cream? Maybe with a

grandparent?



*People who like Jeni's are disgusting folks. Look for someone who appreciates the simple things*

*in life. Hell, a date that enjoys vanilla or chocolate or even cookies and cream is quite alright.*

*You may run into complications down the line with someone who wants a pistachio curry ice*

*cream. Keep on the lookout for these treacherous people and avoid them like the plague.*

Wikimedia Commons

How late do you stay up at night? What's the compatibility in our sleep cycles? I'm not looking

to settle down… but do you really stay up past midnight?

*You do not want to end up with an insomniac. Trust me. That shit gets old really fast.*

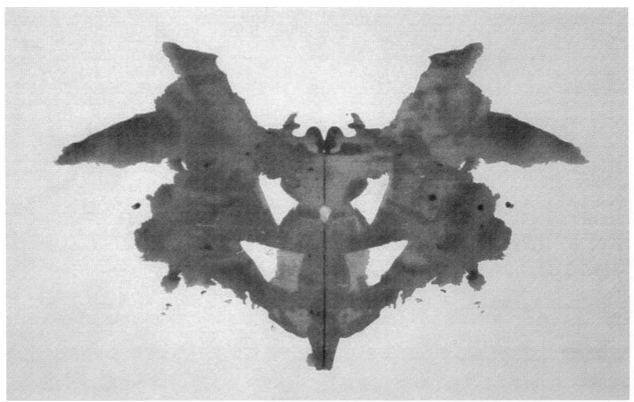

Wikimedia Commons

How did you learn to swim? Can you still swim? Do you think Michael Phelps could beat Ryan Lochte in an arm-wrestling challenge? What if they did it in their speedos? Could you imagine how intense that would be to watch?

*This is a good premise to understand your date's ability to give into temptation. If they squirm a little when you set the scenario in their head, they might have weak mental fortitude to control themselves with a new person. Good to take note.*

Wikimedia Commons

Gunthar Fleck

# General Compatibility

Do you have any pets? What's the weirdest meat you have eaten? Are you a cat person or a dog person?

*These are typical questions asked on a first date given their playfulness. There's no harm in asking and it's always useful to know.*

Wikimedia Commons

Are you a beach person or a mountain person? Would you rather bake in the sun and your own filth all day while limiting your mobility to steps between a cooler and the self-flushing waves of the ocean? Or would you rather tackle a physically demanding obstacle for the valuable views a photo will capture and immediately be buried in an album within a week's time? Or maybe you like exploring cities?

•

*Go ahead and start picturing yourself on vacation with this person. Imagine them in a bathing suit or hiking gear. Really get the juices flowing on longevity and attraction. But do not show them any fidgeting at the sexual thoughts.*

Wikimedia Commons

Did you play any sports in high school? Were you any good? Were you a benchwarmer? If you didn't play any sports, did you have a high school job?

*If they did both, these people have either highly strict parents or are aggressively trying to prove themselves to someone. Huge red flags.*

Wikimedia Commons

What do you do with the pickle spear you get on the side when you order a sandwich from a shop or diner? How do you take your burgers? With bacon? With cheese? What do you prefer as a side? French fries? Side salad?

*This is a concentrated blitzkrieg of compatibility. You want to find someone with eating habits that match yours. Not in the sense that they order similar things, but rather, in a realm in which sharing different items leads to more bang for your buck. If someone shares their pickle, or prefers a cheeseburger, I swear to God you have found the one. Don't think twice.*

Wikimedia Commons

Gunthar Fleck

Did you ever own a KidzBop album? What version are they on now? Perhaps KidzBop 89? Do

you think they have anything provocative out there? You know, something that makes you

question if the producers are even putting in effort or just going through the motions to cash a

paycheck?

*This gives a sense of childhood wonder and shines a light on musical tastes. Bonus points for*

*having an opinion on the decline of the music industry.*

Wikimedia Commons

Did you have an imaginary friend while you were growing up? Were you lonely as well? Do you still hear their voice in your head too? What did you two like to do together?

*A sense of imagination is phenomenal in a partner. Bonus points if your imaginary friend can be buddies with theirs.*

Wikimedia Commons

Were you a Backstreet Boys or N'Sync kid? At what point in your life were they transformative to you? Do you think you would have found music the same if it weren't for their influence on your life? Who were your favorite members?

*Understanding early age music and boy band obsessions is essential for categorizing your date's identity of themselves. Let's hope they're old enough to draw a parallel to your boy band days. And don't settle for anyone with the stock answer of Justin Timberlake being their favorite boy-band member. You are better than that.*

Wikimedia Commons

What is your go-to karaoke song? How many drinks does it take to get you on stage? Why is 1980's dance music so contagious? Did you know Tiffany who sings "I Think We're Alone Now" had stalkers? Have you seen her documentary?

*Having fun is key to being happy in life. If things get dull after some time, there is nothing wrong with taking your date to a karaoke bar. If anything, it gives you leverage to have another date with them assuming you want to. Suggest it.*

Wikimedia Commons

Would you rather eat your favorite fast food for the rest of your life, or would you rather keep a

healthy hairline and trim figure for the rest of your life?

*This helps weed out the liars. No normal, self-respecting person would maintain an alliance to*

*fitness over familiar, cheap cravings. Huge red flag.*

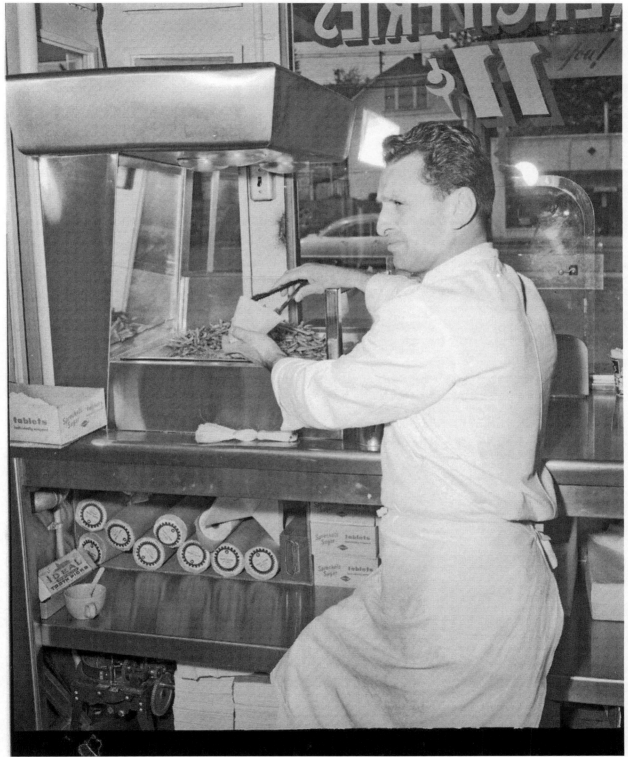

Wikimedia Commons

Would you eat in a restaurant alone? What about go to a movie alone? What is it about seeing people out by themselves that gives off a general sense of sadness? Do you think there is someone for everyone?

*Asking this is a good measure of your date's independence. You want someone to be independent enough, but not some sort of monster who could live without anyone for the rest of their days. Try to gather an idea if they are available enough for you.*

Wikimedia Commons

Gunthar Fleck

# Things to Know

Are both your grandparents still alive? If one or all of them have passed away, did they leave behind any wisdom? Did they leave behind anything scandalous? Any hidden families? Any good recipes that may have been passed down?

*Knowing family history is intriguing. If this person is going to be your partner, you will want to know all about their genetics and drama.*

Wikimedia Commons

What was the weirdest job you've ever worked? Was it the task or the boss or the time of day

that made it so bizarre? What was the pay? Was it more or less money than you make now? Who

got you the job?


*Asking questions about work and pay shows that you respect contributions to the productivity of*

*society.*

Wikimedia Commons

Are you a gambling person? Have you ever walked away from a casino making money? If so, would you want to make our next date to a casino and pool our money together? How well do you tip your dealer?

*These people contemplated going on a date with you, so, regardless of their answer, they are all gamblers. Maybe you'll find someone funny to crack a joke about taking a risk on you. Maybe you will find someone to blow some travel credits on a trip to Vegas with you. But, despite the pretense, the questions logically point out people with problems and happy go lucky folks. This is indicative of a "read between the lines" type of moment. Hopefully you make the right choice.*

Wikimedia Commons

How did your parents meet? What is their age difference? Are they still together? Which parent do you prefer more? Do you look like either one of them? If so, can I see a picture?

*The idea of marriage is a respectful one. How they answer this provides a good glimpse in their upbringing and whether they have a similar family life as you. It is also ideal to know what your date could look like in their old age.*

Wikimedia Commons

Do you make your bed each day? Is it freeing to get into a bed that is the same as you left it at your most comfortable? Or do you find it comforting to get into a bed that you will ruin through a night of tossing and turning? What do you put under your pillow each night in hopes that you wake up with a gift from a sleep fairy? How often do you flip your mattress?

*Inside a person exists a barbaric spectrum. Obvious to little, but people who make their beds look to destroy things within their control. If you show one sign of weakness, this bed maker is going to demolish you at the right moment.*

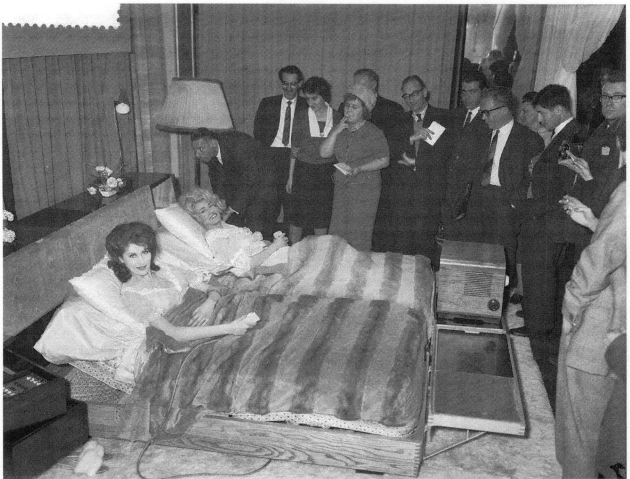

Wikimedia Commons

Gunthar Fleck

How was your pandemic? Did you do anything fun during quarantine? How many times have

you caught COVID? What did you think of Tiger King? How good is the bread you learned how

to make?

*This opens a door for a person to become political or vulnerable. Pay attention closely as the*

*indicator they give could be a deal breaker. Mostly, we are just looking for someone who*

*downloaded TikTok and keeps track of the latest trends post-COVID lockdown.*

Wikimedia Commons

Gunthar Fleck

# A Brief History of the First Date

For a little history, the first "first date" was recorded around 400 A.D. because every relationship before then was decided by not the suitors, but by the parents for favorable property gain. In Athens, Greece, during the Byzantine Empire, it was decreed by the governing Roman Church that independence in romantic affairs should take societal form. This was encouraged for economic purposes as drought and diseases had wiped out civilizations within the sovereign nation. The goal was to reflect an autonomous free-will state popular with the advancement in ideologies for the purpose of procreation that would lead to a growing economy and military empowerment.

Within the once budding counterculture dregs of the civilization, a young man named Sycadus caught the eye of the town's precocious basket weaver, Dyloria. She was a looker too. Sycadus took one glance at Dyloria and decided enough was enough with his ways of youth; it was time for him to settle down. The Church, while archaic in its age of 100 years, might be on to something with their radical new ideas. Not to mention, he was also getting a little tired from his late night's out with the rest of his rabblerousing group of guys. In a moment of swift courage, he approached the young Dyloria and requested her attendance at the weekly symposium. It was weird to ask and not demand, but he was all for every individual's autonomy. Something about it felt more equitable. It was almost as if she had rights equivalent to his. Her eyes fluttered at the question, and she answered him with a resilient "Sure".

The days leading up to their rendezvous filled Sycadus with tummy demons as the local medicine men referred to what we now call "butterflies". He was nervous about what he would say. Or how she would react to his quirky personality. He wrote down with chisel on a slate all sorts of questions he could ask Dyloria. But in the end, he decided to leave those marble tablets back home. When the day came, Sycadus questioned if he should even go to the symposium. He could send his friend, Textius, to deliver her a message saying he had something come up. But in the end, he really wanted to see her. He faced his reflection in a shallow puddle of chariot horse urine and told himself he could do this. And did it he did. He picked up Dyloria from her basket weaving post in the market and walked her toward the Agora where the symposium was scheduled. The two made off like bandits. Laughing arm in arm, they circled the pillars of Athens adoring one another. Sycadus realized he had nothing to be worried about because Dyloria would not have given him the time of day had she not found him charming. There was a mutual agreement by the two of them that a date would be pretty chill. And with that, the couple went on to live the rest of their old lives for the next 15 years where they died of natural causes in their 40's.

The moral of the story is that you do not need to worry about first dates. Leading up to it, you can be filled with so many "what-ifs". The best way to approach these anxieties is to memorize the previous questions and capitalize on the short time you have on your first date. Use the time leading up to the date to brush up on these significant queries. That way you can be prepared. And, as the date approaches, keep your eyes on the finish line. Do not worry about judgement, just worry about which one of you will die first after a happy marriage. You better hope it's not you!

Gunthar Fleck

Wikimedia Commons

# Let Me Walk You Back To Your Car

And just like any date, we have come to an end. If it was any good, you might have fallen asleep with your arm around it. Even if it was bad, you have a story and a receipt to prove you had the experience. Pleasurable or not, maybe you had some laughs, hopefully you didn't cry, or even worse, discarded it in the trash once you found it worthless to any societal contribution. The thing is, I found you charming for even picking me out of a crowd. And you, you may have found the book interesting or, at the very least, something to make your parents question your taste. Regardless, let's be real and say we are one and done. That is, until late at night, when we get the craving to pick each other up, a reunion occurs in which the fascination and excitement is relived at a fraction of the first time. It doesn't matter, we can convince ourselves it's just a fling. But there I am, years later, still sitting on your coffee table. A cornerstone of your living room at this point. Your friends know me. Some roll their eyes. And the few that engage, we secretly like. Thanks for picking me up, sweetie. Next time we'll go Dutch ;)

# **About the Author**

Gunthar is the author of "Raised By A Glass" which is a memoir that focuses on the cocktails that have been formative to his life and the stories that accompany them. Over the course of his career, Gunthar has written not only an impressive number of emails as a Finance professional, but volumes of creative writing that unceremoniously found its way to a trashcan on Chicago's Blue Line and much more conceived since that devastating moment. His popularity comes from a Yelp review of the local "Rock N' Roll" McDonalds which has been a critical masterpiece in the underground of Chicago's River North Neighborhood.

Gunthar lives in Chicago by way of Atlanta. He draws on artistic influences from a multitude of mediums including Nelson Algren, Father John Misty, Anthony Bourdain, Mark Normand, and Jonah Hill. When he is not working or writing you can find him at a neighborhood bar. He will either be playing Skee Ball, talking to regulars, or introvertedly enjoying a gin and tonic.